Wildlife Watching

Bear Watching

by Diane Bair and Pamela Wright

Consultant:
Charles Jonkel
Scientific Editor/Advisor
Great Bear Foundation

CAPSTONE BOOKS
an imprint of Capstone Press
Mankato, Minnesota

Capstone Books are published by Capstone Press
P.O. Box 669, 151 Good Counsel Drive, Mankato, Minnesota 56002
http://www.capstone-press.com

Library of Congress Cataloging-in-Publication Data
Bair, Diane.
    Bear watching/by Diane Bair and Pamela Wright.
    p. cm.—(Wildlife watching)
    Includes bibliographical references and index.
    Summary: Describes the physical characteristics and habits of bears, different
species, and how to safely observe them.
    ISBN 0-7368-0319-X
    1. Bear watching—Juvenile literature. [1. Bear watching. 2. Bears.] I. Wright,
Pamela, 1953– . II. Title. III. Series: Bair, Diane. Wildlife watching.
QL737.C27B3455 2000
599.78—DC21   99-19585
                                                              CIP

Editorial Credits
Carrie A. Braulick, editor; Steve Christensen, cover designer and illustrator;
    Heidi Schoof, photo researcher

Photo Credits
David F. Clobes, cover inset, 14, 18, 23, 38
Dominique Braud/TOM STACK & ASSOCIATES, 8
John Shaw/TOM STACK & ASSOCIATES, 45
Photo Network/Bachmann, 7; Howard Folsom, 10; Mark Newman, 32
Photri, 34
Robert McCaw, 17, 37, 40
Root Resources/Mary & Lloyd McCarthy, 42
Thomas Kitchin/TOM STACK & ASSOCIATES, 26, 41
Unicorn Stock Photos/Ron Holt, cover
Visuals Unlimited/Tom Edwards, 4; Carlyn Galati, 13; Jan L. Wassink, 21;
    Gerald & Buff Corsi, 28

**Thank you to Lynn Rogers, North American Bear Center, for his assistance in
preparing this book.**

Table of Contents

Chapter 1

Getting to Know Bears

People have always been fascinated with the size and strength of bears. Ancient Romans used bears for sport. They put a bear and another animal in an arena. People gathered to watch the two animals fight. In the 1700s and 1800s, people trained bears in Europe. People paid the trainers to watch the bears' tricks. Today, you can learn how to watch bears safely in other ways. You also can learn about the signs bears leave behind in areas where they live.

Bears have great size and strength.

About Bears

Eight types of bears live in the world. Each type of bear is called a species. Each bear species has a different range. This is the geographic region where a plant or animal species naturally lives. The ranges of black bears, brown bears, and polar bears include parts of North America.

All bear species share some common features. Thick fur covers their bodies. Bears have large heads with rounded ears. Bears have five long claws on each paw. They use these claws to dig, climb, and catch other animals to eat.

All bears have an excellent sense of smell. Some scientists believe brown bears can smell a scent from one mile (1.6 kilometers) away.

Scientists place all bears in a group called carnivores. Animals in this group eat meat. But some bears also eat large amounts of plant material. These bears include black bears, brown bears, and pandas.

Bears are carnivores.

Brown bears are called grizzly bears because they have gray-tipped fur.

Bear species also differ in some ways. Their sizes vary. Sun bears are the world's smallest bears. Sun bears weigh about 100 pounds (45 kilograms). Polar bears are the world's largest bears. Polar bears can weigh more than 1,500 pounds (680 kilograms).

Bears vary in color. They can be shades of brown. They also can be black, tan, cream, or white. Most bears are one color. But some bears are more than one color. For example, pandas are black and white.

Brown bears also are called grizzly bears. Their gray-tipped fur gives them a grizzled appearance.

Bears of one species are not always the same color. For example, not all brown bears are brown. They can be tan or black. Not all black bears are black. They can be light or dark brown. They even can be white, cream, blue-gray, or orange-brown. White and cream-colored black bears are called kermode bears. They live only in certain parts of British Columbia, Canada.

Home Ranges

Bears have home ranges. Bears look for food in these areas. Male bears also look for mates in their home ranges.

The size of a bear's home range depends on the amount of food available. Bears living in areas with plenty of food have small home

ranges. For example, brown bears that live near an ocean often catch a large amount of fish. Their home ranges may be only about 10 square miles (26 square kilometers). Other brown bears live in areas where food is scarce. These bears may have home ranges as large as 500 square miles (1,295 square kilometers).

Home ranges of male bears often are larger than those of females. Male bears often travel farther to find mates. Female black bears usually have home ranges of 2.5 to 10 square miles (6.5 to 26 square kilometers). Male black bears usually have home ranges of 10 to 40 square miles (26 to 104 square kilometers).

Polar bears have the largest home ranges. They often travel several hundred miles to find food. Some polar bears have home ranges of more than 200,000 square miles (518,000 square kilometers).

Polar bears have the largest home ranges.

Bear Behavior

Some people think that bears are aggressive. They believe bears usually attack people. But this is not true. Bears usually avoid people. They move or hide if they sense people are near.

Bears may attack people in certain situations. For example, bears sometimes do not sense people are near. The wind may blow people's scents away from bears. Bears may then be surprised if people get too close to them. Surprised bears may attack.

Bears have personal spaces. Bears guard these areas around them. Some bears guard large spaces. Female bears with cubs may guard an area that extends 150 yards (137 meters) around them. These bears are protecting their cubs. Other bears guard smaller areas. Brown bears that are used to people may guard spaces about 60 yards (55 meters) away.

Some bear species are more aggressive than other bear species. For example, brown bears

Bears with cubs may be more aggressive than other bears.

usually are more aggressive than black bears. Black bears are more likely to run away when people come near places where they live.

Bears also closely guard their food. They may become aggressive if other animals or people approach them while they are eating.

Keep bear behavior in mind when you go bear watching. This will help keep you safe.

Chapter 2

Preparing for Your Adventure

You can go bear watching in two ways. You can watch live bears at special viewing areas. You also can look for bear signs in areas where bears live. These signs include bear tracks and tree markings. Bears may strip bark from trees or make claw marks on them.

Learn about bears before you go bear watching. Check out books about bears from your school or local library. Look for web sites about bears on the Internet. Ask rangers for information about bears. Rangers are in charge of parks or forests. They often teach people about bears that live in these areas.

You can talk to rangers to learn about bears.

Viewing Areas

You may choose to watch bears at viewing areas. Some national parks and wildlife refuges have these areas. Guides may take you on tours at these places. Guides can show you where and how to view bears safely. They may take you to viewing platforms. You can watch bears from these platforms. Some viewing platforms are high above the ground. You also may view bears from shelters or other safe places.

Most viewing areas have rules that you must follow. Some only allow a few visitors at a time to observe the bears. You may have to buy permits or pay a fee. You may have to stay on viewing platforms or marked trails and paths.

Learn when you can visit viewing areas. Some areas only are open during certain times of the year. Try to visit viewing areas in the morning or evening. Bears are more active during these times of the day.

You may visit a viewing area to observe bears safely.

What to Bring to Viewing Areas

Bring binoculars to viewing areas. This viewing tool makes distant objects appear closer. You can observe bear features and behaviors from a safe distance with binoculars.

You may want to keep records of your bear watching experiences. Bring items to record information. These may include a notebook, sketch pad, and camera.

Bring a camera with a telephoto lens if you can. Telephoto lenses work like binoculars. They make distant objects appear closer. You also may bring a video camera. You can keep detailed recordings of your observations with a video camera.

Wear proper clothing to special viewing areas. Comfortable pants and long-sleeved shirts are best. These clothes help protect you from insect bites. Bring a jacket. Wear sturdy shoes or boots so you can walk easier on rocky or weedy paths. Dress warmly if you go to viewing areas during cold weather. Wear a hat, gloves, and boots.

Looking for Bear Signs

You may want to search for bear signs in areas where bears live. These areas include national parks and wildlife refuges. Some people call these areas "bear country."

You can find a variety of signs in bear country. You may find tree markings, tracks, or bear droppings. Bear droppings also are called scat.

You may want to bring a camera and other supplies to viewing areas.

Look for black and brown bear signs during spring, summer, and fall. Black and brown bears are most active during August and September.

Bear signs may be difficult to find during winter. Black and brown bears hibernate during winter. They go into a deep sleep in dens. These sleeping places may be in caves or hollow trees. Bears become active again in spring. Do not disturb bears in dens. Hibernating bears that are awakened may lose energy they need to survive until spring.

Look for bear signs during late morning or early afternoon. Bears usually rest during mid-day. You are less likely to encounter bears during this time. Bears hunt and eat during early mornings and evenings. Bears that are busy eating may not sense you. They may become surprised.

What to Bring to Look for Bear Signs

Bring items to record the signs you see. You may bring a camera, notebook, and pens or pencils. You also can bring a ruler to measure bear tracks.

Bears hibernate in dens during winter.

You can make casts of bear tracks with plaster of paris. You mix this white powder with water. It then forms a paste that dries quickly and hardens. You can buy plaster of paris at most art supply or craft stores.

You may choose to set up a campsite when you look for bear signs. You must take extra care with any food you bring. Bring only low-odor food. Do not leave food out or cook foods with strong smells. This may attract bears. Keep food in airtight containers and store it away from other camping items. Some parks and wildlife refuges have special bear-safe food storage boxes. Garbage also can attract bears. Keep garbage in airtight containers. Carry it out when you leave bear country.

Do not bring food when you leave your campsite to walk on trails. The food's smell may attract bears. But you may want to bring a water bottle.

Wear proper clothes to look for bear signs. Wear long pants and long-sleeved shirts. This will help protect you from insect bites and scratches from branches. Do not wear clothes that smell like food. Change into different clothes after you cook food. Bears may smell the food scent on your clothes and approach you.

Any strong-smelling items may attract bears. Do not wear scented products such as deodorant and perfume.

You may want to set up a campsite when you look for bear signs.

Safety in Bear Country

1. Let bears know you are near. Most bears then will know you are coming and move away. Talk in a normal voice. You may clap or call out. This helps bears hear you. Some people bring bells or horns into bear country.

2. Try to walk in the same direction the wind is blowing. This helps bears smell you. Do not walk upwind on trails in heavily wooded areas.

3. Always go to bear country with at least one other person. This person should be an adult. Adults can guide children and help them look for bear signs. It is best to visit bear country in groups. Groups make more noise than one or two people. Bears rarely attack people in large groups.

4. Remain calm if you see a bear from a distance. Talk in a normal voice. Wave your arms slowly so the bear can see you. Try to leave the bear a way to escape. Turn around and leave. You also may wait for the bear to leave if it is distant from you.

5. Never approach bears. This may surprise them. Bears also guard personal spaces around them.

6. Never feed bears. These bears may learn to seek more food from people. Some of these bears may become aggressive.

7. Do not come between a female bear and her cubs. Female bears protect their cubs.

8. Stay on marked trails. Never follow fresh bear signs. Do not wander into heavily wooded areas. Do not walk near noisy streams. Bears may not hear you.

9. Camp in open areas away from berry patches, streams, lakes, and dead animals. Set up your cooking and eating area at least 300 feet (91 meters) from your sleeping area. Do not sleep in the same clothes you cook in.

10. Place all food and garbage in airtight, bear-safe containers. Parks sometimes supply these containers. Keep personal items with odors in bear-safe containers. Items such as deodorant, soap, lotion, and toothpaste may attract bears. You also may hang these items from a tree branch. Make sure your bags are at least 10 feet (3 meters) above the ground and 4 feet (1.2 meters) from the tree trunk. This will prevent bears from reaching your bags if they climb the tree. Store cooking clothes with food and items that have odors.

11. Do not disturb bears in dens or at any other time.

Follow these guidelines if you do encounter a bear at close range: Back up very slowly. Never stare at a bear. Look to the side. Do not growl. Do not run away from a bear. The bear may follow you.

Chapter 3

Where to Look

You may see bears and bear signs in their habitats. These are the natural places and conditions in which bears live. Black and brown bears have habitats in river valleys, forests, and meadows. Polar bears live on the ice in Arctic areas.

Bear Signs at Feeding Areas

You can find black and brown bear signs near their feeding areas. Black and brown bears eat berries, plants, roots, and nuts. They sometimes eat insects, birds, and fish. Look for black and brown bear signs near berry trees, streams, and rivers. Look near flowers and other plants. Black bears eat a large amount of plant material during spring. They sometimes eat a thin, sweet

Bears spend much of their time near their feeding areas.

layer of cells under tree bark called cambium. Look near decaying logs. Black and brown bears sometimes eat insects that live in these logs.

You can find a variety of bear signs at their feeding areas. You may see bear tracks or tree markings. You also may find a bear's day bed. Bears sometimes rest in these places during the day. Bears may trample plants or dig shallow pits in the ground to make day beds.

Do not wander off marked trails to look for bear signs. You may surprise bears or enter their personal spaces.

Public Viewing Areas

You can watch black and brown bears in many viewing areas. Some of these areas are in the United States and Canada. Many viewing areas are in national parks or wildlife refuges.

One of the best places to view polar bears is in Churchill, Manitoba, Canada. Polar bears gather near this town in the fall. They wait for the ice to freeze on Hudson Bay. They then go out on the ice to hunt seals.

Bears sometimes eat cambium from trees. You may find bear scratches on these trees.

Places to See Bears

1 **Katmai National Park and Preserve,
near King Salmon, Alaska:**
More brown bears per square mile live in this park than in any other
place in the world. These bears fish for salmon in Brooks River.
Visitors watch the bears from a viewing platform located near the
river. The best bear-viewing months are July and September.

2 **Vince Shute Wildlife Sanctuary,
Orr, Minnesota:**
Visitors can view black bears from late May until early September.
Visitors watch bears from a viewing platform located in a 2-acre
(.8 hectare) opening in the forest.

3 **Grizzly Discovery Center,
Yellowstone National Park, West Yellowstone, Montana:**
Visitors can observe brown bears here year-round. These bears
often stay active during the winter because food is available
during this time. The bears are in an area enclosed by a fence.
Visitors may watch the bears from areas outside the fence.

4 **Churchill,
Manitoba, Canada:**
Polar bears gather near this town to wait for the ice to freeze on
Hudson Bay. They roam near the shore. The bears go on the ice to
hunt seals after the ice freezes. Visitors can see the bears from
September to early November. They view the bears from large
buses called "tundra buggies."

5 **Anan Wildlife Observatory,
Tongass National Forest, near Wrangell, Alaska:**
Visitors can view black and brown bears at this observatory. The
bears fish for salmon in the Anan Creek. Visitors can view the bears
from an open-sided shelter near the creek. July and August are the
best times to view these bears.

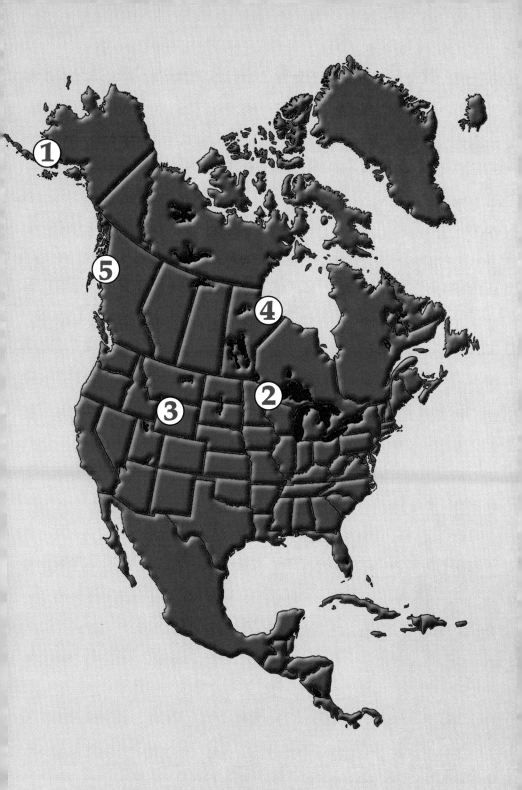

Chapter 4

Making Observations

You can make many different observations about bears and bear signs. You may watch bears search for food or play together at viewing areas. You may note different features about bear signs.

Tracks

Look for bear tracks when you search for bear signs. Bears' hind leg tracks look similar to people's footprints. Bears and people both have five toes. But bears' big toes are on the outsides of their feet. Bears' feet touch the ground much like people's feet. Both their

You can observe bear behavior at viewing areas.

heels and toes hit the ground. You may notice small holes in front of some bear tracks. Brown bears' sharp front claws often make these holes. Brown bears' claws can be up to 4.5 inches (11 centimeters) long.

Observe the space between bear tracks. Bears sometimes move very quickly. They may chase small animals. Quickly moving bears leave more space between their tracks. Bears that walk slowly leave tracks that are closer together.

You may be able to tell what type of bear made tracks. Brown bears usually have larger tracks than black bears. Brown bear tracks usually are about 11 inches (28 centimeters) long. Black bear tracks usually are 6 to 7 inches (15 to 18 centimeters) long.

Look at the toes of bear tracks. The toes of black bears' front tracks form a curved line. Grizzly bears' front toes form a straighter line.

Tree Markings

Look carefully at trees along trails. Bears often leave marks on trees. Bears sometimes rub up

Bears that walk slowly leave tracks that are close together.

against trees. Bears rub their shoulders, backs, and heads on trees. You may find patches of hair or a few hairs stuck on trees.

Bears also claw and bite trees. You may see bark stripped from the bases of trees. Bears scratch off bark from trees for food. They may scratch logs to eat the worms or insects inside. You may see bears' toothmarks in trees. Many male black and brown bears bite trees during mating season. These bears mate between May and July.

Bear Scat

Look for bear scat. Bear scat is usually dark brown or black. It looks similar to dog droppings. But bear scat is a little larger than most dog droppings.

You may poke at bear scat with a stick. This will help you learn what the bear has been eating. Black and brown bear scat often contains grass and roots during spring. Bear scat also may contain animal hair, nuts, or berries. Never touch bear scat with your hands. This may spread disease.

Bears tear apart logs to look for insects.

Recording Your Observations

You may want to record your observations of bears and bear signs. This will help you keep track of your bear watching experiences.

You may take notes about bears at viewing areas. Note bears' behavior. Write down the bears' colors. You may want to draw or photograph bears. You can take video recordings of bears.

You also may record bear signs. Draw or photograph tree markings. Collect bear hair from trees. You may want to measure bear tracks with a ruler. Measure the sizes of the tracks and the distance between each track.

You can mix plaster of paris with water to make casts of bear tracks. Place a small amount of the plaster in the tracks. Wait about 10 minutes until the mixture hardens. Then dig the cast out.

Make recordings about bears each time you go bear watching. This will help you remember your experiences for years to come.

You may want to record your observations of bears and bear signs in a notebook.

Black Bear

Description: Black bears are the most common bears in North America. Most of these bears are black. Some are a shade of brown. White and cream black bears live in British Columbia, Canada. These bears are called kermode bears. Most black bears have brown muzzles.

Black bears are about 4.5 to 6 feet (1.4 to 1.8 meters) long. Adult males usually weigh 130 to 600 pounds (59 to 272 kilograms). Adult females usually weigh 90 to 300 pounds (41 to 136 kilograms). The largest black bear ever recorded weighed more than 800 pounds (363 kilograms). Black bears' weights often depend on the amount of available food.

Black bears are fast climbers. They can climb a tree as fast as a squirrel can. Their short, curved claws help them climb trees. Black bears often climb trees when they sense danger. Black bears can run up to 40 miles (64 kilometers) per hour. Black bears usually are less aggressive than brown bears.

Habitat: Forests, swamps

Food: Plants, berries, dead animals, insects, acorns, honey, salmon

■ = Range

Brown Bear

Description: Brown bears of interior North America are called grizzly bears. North American brown bears that live near ocean coasts sometimes are called coastal brown bears. Grizzly bears have gray-tipped or "grizzled" fur. Most brown bears are brown. They also may be tan, black, or orange-red.

Brown bears are larger than black bears. They are about 6.5 to 7 feet (2 to 2.1 meters) long. Some may be more than 10 feet (3 meters) long. Adult males usually weigh 300 to 860 pounds (136 to 390 kilograms). Adult females usually weigh 200 to 450 pounds (91 to 204 kilograms). Brown bears that live near large bodies of water can weigh more than 1,500 pounds (680 kilograms). These bears have plenty of fish to eat.

Brown bears can run 30 to 40 miles (48 to 64 kilometers) per hour. Brown bears are threatened throughout most of the United States. This means they are in danger of dying out.

Habitat: Forests, open meadows, near river valleys and streams

Food: Plants, salmon, deer, insects, dead animals, berries

= Range

Polar Bear

Description: Polar bears are the largest of all bears. They also are the world's largest land carnivores. Polar bears are white or yellow-white. They are about 8.25 to 11.5 feet (2.5 to 3.5 meters) long. Adult males usually weigh 880 to 1,320 pounds (399 to 599 kilograms). But some may weigh more than 1,500 pounds (680 kilograms). Adult females usually weigh 440 to 660 pounds (200 to 299 kilograms). Polar bears have thick layers of fat to keep them warm. This fat can be 4.5 inches (11 centimeters) thick.

Polar bears are excellent divers and swimmers. Polar bears have long necks to help them keep their heads above water as they swim. They also have webbed forepaws to help them swim. Polar bears' forepaws are larger than their hind paws. Polar bears use their forepaws to help push their bodies through water. Polar bears have two layers of fur. Their outer layer of fur is hollow. This helps polar bears stay afloat in the water. Polar bears can swim more than 60 miles (96 kilometers) without stopping to rest.

Habitat: Northern Arctic regions

Food: Seals, walruses, dead whales; some seaweed and berries

■ = **Land Range**

■ = **Ice Range**

Words to Know

cambium (CAM-bee-um)—a thin, sweet layer of cells under the bark of trees

carnivore (CAR-nuh-vor)—an animal that eats meat

day bed (DAY BED)—a place where a bear rests during the day

habitat (HAB-uh-tat)—the places and natural conditions in which an animal lives

hibernate (HYE-bur-nate)—to spend the winter in a deep sleep

home range (HOME RAYNJ)—the area in which a bear travels to find food and mates

range (RAYNJ)—geographic region where a plant or animal species naturally lives

scat (SKAT)—animal droppings

species (SPEE-sheez)—a group of a certain kind of animal with similar features; black bears are one species of bear.

To Learn More

Brown, Gary. *Safe Travel in Bear Country.* New York: Lyons and Burford, 1996.

Hemstock, Annie. *The Polar Bear.* Wildlife of North America. Mankato, Minn.: Capstone High/Low Books, 1999.

Hunt, Joni Phelps. *Bears.* Close Up. Parsippany, N.J.: Silver Burdett Ginn, 1995.

Murray, John A. *Grizzly Bears: An Illustrated Field Guide.* Boulder, Colo.: Roberts Rinehart Publishers, 1995.

Potts, Steve. *The Grizzly Bear.* Wildlife of North America. Mankato, Minn.: Capstone High/Low Books, 1999.

Russo, Monica. *Watching Nature: A Beginner's Field Guide.* New York: Sterling Publishing, 1998.

Useful Addresses

Alaska Department of Fish and Game
P.O. Box 25526
Juneau, AK 99802-5526

Animal Alliance of Canada
221 Broadview Avenue
Suite 101
Toronto, ON M4M 2G3
Canada

The Great Bear Foundation
P.O. Box 9383
Missoula, MT 59807

North American Bear Center
P.O. Box 161
Ely, MN 55731

Internet Sites

The Bear Den
http://www.nature-net.com/bears

Bears of North America
http://www.montana.com/rattlesnake

Bear Taxon Advisory Group's Bear Den
http://www.bearden.org/index.html

Katmai National Park and Preserve
http://www.nps.gov/katm

North American Bear Center
http://bear.org

World Wildlife Fund–Canada
http://www.wwfcanada.org

Index